Sea Shells and Weddin

Illustrations: Jenny Williams
Writer: Siân Lewis

Plasyfelin Primary School

Concept, creation and design by FBA Publications in association with the
Qualifications, Curriculum & Assessment Authority (ACCAC)
FBA Publications
Aberystwyth
2001

Bethan and Gareth were on holiday at the seaside with Mam and Dad.
Gareth was digging a hole and Bethan was collecting shells.
She liked the tiny pink ones best, because they looked like little mouse ears.

Bethan had only half-filled her bucket when it started to rain.
'Never mind,' said Mam.
'You can look for more shells tomorrow.
Let's run back to the caravan to get our jackets,
then we'll drive into Porthmadog to do some shopping.'

All the other holidaymakers had had the same idea.
Bethan spotted two friends from the caravan site
in the doorway of a book shop.

While Mam went to buy bread,
Dad, Bethan and Gareth walked over to the marina.
'Look, that boat's got my name on it,' shouted Bethan.

Mam came back with fish and chips for lunch.
They ate them in the car.
'Mm! I enjoyed that,' said Dad, as he started the engine.
'Now, if you look to your left when we drive out
of town,' said Mam, 'you'll see Snowdon,
the highest mountain in Wales.'
Bethan and Gareth pressed their noses against the
window and looked at the mountains in the distance.
But the top of Snowdon was lost in the clouds.

'Can we go to the top?' Gareth asked.
'Not today,' said Dad with a smile.
'It's too wet. But we could go **into** a mountain instead.'
'We're going to visit a slate mine,' said Mam, passing Dad
five pence to pay the man at the tollgate just outside Porthmadog.

As soon as Dad parked the car at Llechwedd Slate Mine,
the rain stopped and the sun came out.
The slate and rooftops sparkled all around.
'Let's see how they used to mine slate in the old days,' said Mam
leading the way towards the museum.

8

In the museum Gareth noticed large slabs of slate.
'What did they do with these big stones
once they'd dug them out?' he asked.
'They split them into thin slices and put them
on the roofs of houses,' replied Bethan.
'Just think," said Mam, 'ships used to sail from
Porthmadog and take Welsh slates all over the world.'

9

Gareth and Bethan couldn't wait to go underground.
They put on hard hats and joined the long line of people
waiting to visit Deep Mine.
The train took them slowly down to the start of their walk
through the cold, dark, damp caves, deep inside the mountain.

Suddenly they came across a huge cave.
As the lights grew brighter they could see a still lake.
'It's like magic!' whispered Bethan, as the cave filled with
red and green and blue lights ... and beautiful music.
But the show was soon over.
'Can't we go around again?' asked Gareth
as they made their way back up to the open air.

On the way back to the car, Bethan and Gareth bought souvenirs.
Bethan chose a slate key-ring for her collection
and Gareth bought a yellow plastic hard hat.
'I'm going to be a builder when I grow up,' he said.
'What are you going to build?' asked Bethan.
'Anything I like,' Gareth said, playing with the
little slate bits he had picked up in the cave.

'We'll have to take you to Portmeirion then,' said Dad later, as he drove back to the caravan site along the twisty road. 'You'll really like it there. It's a whole village built by just one man, Clough Williams-Ellis, who filled it with all sorts of buildings that took his fancy.'

The next day, when they went to Portmeirion,
Gareth was still wearing his yellow hat.
In Portmeirion there were houses and shops the same colour as his hat -
and pink ones and blue ones of all shapes and sizes.

14

'When I grow up, I'm going to build a tower like that,'
said Gareth, pointing at a tall spiky building with a bell inside.
'I want to build a lake and a statue like that,' said Bethan.

15

Mam took hold of her hand and pointed to a wedding party
standing on the other side of the lake.
The group was waiting to have photographs taken,
and the breeze was blowing the bridesmaids' dresses.
'Aren't they lucky that the sun is shining?' said Dad.
'Yesterday they could have got soaking wet.'

Gareth had wandered off and was standing staring at a silent stone lion.
Bethan crept quietly up behind him and roared loudly in his ear.
Gareth jumped out of his skin.

Then, all of a sudden they heard people shouting.
'I think they're looking for someone,' said Bethan.

Out of the blue a small boy dressed like a sailor
darted out from the nearby bushes.
'Quick, quick!' whispered Bethan as she turned to her left.
'We'd better help catch him.'
The two of them chased after him as fast as they could.

Bethan grabbed the small pageboy
and steered him back towards the wedding party.
Everyone crowded around to thank Bethan for finding him.
'Well, well,' said her dad. 'What a to-do! This is definitely worth a picture!'

By the time they got back to the caravan later,
the sun was setting.

20

Gareth lined up his postcards of Portmeirion
and got into bed with his hat on.
'I really do wish I could build a village,' he said.
'I wish I didn't have to wait till I'm grown up.'
'Well, you don't have to wait,' said Bethan
and she whispered in his ear.

21

The next morning Gareth and Bethan went down to the beach straight after breakfast. With Mam and Dad's help they built two little villages in the sand.

THIS BEACH IS ZONED
MAE'R TRAETH HWN WEDI EI RANNU'N BARTHAU

In Port-Gareth there was a river and a ship and a castle with slates on its roof.
And in Port-Bethan there was a lake and a garden made of shells.

Geography Consultant: Olive Dyer

British Library Cataloguing-in-Publication Data.

A catalogue record for this publication is available from the
British Library.

Published with the financial assistance of ACCAC (The Qualifications,
Curriculum & Assessment Authority for Wales).

Published July 2001 by
FBA Publications, Number 4, The Science Park
Aberystwyth, Ceredigion SY23 3AH
Tel: (01970) 636411 Fax: (01970) 636414
Email: publishing@fbagroup.co.uk
Web: www.fbagroup.co.uk

Designed by Francis Balsom Associates
Printed in Wales

ISBN 1 901862 47 X

Plasyfelin Primary School